Blooming Into Your Purpose
BREAKING THROUGH

Foreword by
Cris Meadows

La Deema Burns

Pearly Gates Publishing LLC, Houston, Texas

Blooming Into Your Purpose
Breaking Through

Copyright © 2016
La Deema Burns

All Rights Reserved.
No portion of this publication may be reproduced, stored in any electronic system, or transmitted in any form or by any means (electronic, mechanical, photocopy, recording, or otherwise) without written permission from the publisher. Brief quotations may be used in literary reviews.

ISBN 13: 978-1945117145
ISBN 10: 1945117141
Library of Congress Control Number: 2016942704

For information and bulk ordering, contact:
Pearly Gates Publishing LLC
Angela R. Edwards, CEO
P.O. Box 62287
Houston, TX 77205
BestSeller@PearlyGatesPublishing.com

What Others Are Saying

"La Deema Burns is an awesome woman of God. She both encourages and challenges you to walk towards and in your purpose in a way that is loving and intentional. I am thankful to God for her encouragement, support, and all that she is doing to honor and bring increase to the Kingdom of God."

~ Andrea Smith

"My sister and my friend, La Deema Burns, is walking in her purpose. How do I know? Simply because I am walking in mine. God has divinely-connected us together. She is the Owner of a radio platform – iBloom Radio. She is also an Author and Life Coach. La Deema is allowing her past to propel her into her present and onward into her future. She is not allowing the spirit of fear to derail her from her purpose. I am very, very proud of the work she is doing and the life she is purposely living."

~ Dr. Walter Sims

"La Deema Burns has blessed my life tremendously in the short time I've known her. She saw gifts inside of me that I didn't know I possessed. She took me – a small seed – and nourished me by speaking life into my soul. She didn't **PUSH** me into my purpose; she **PULLED** me into it. She's on who really takes her people by the hand and walks with them on their journey into their destined places. She's an awesome mentor and producer. La Deema is truly a one-of-a-kind blessing. Today, I am "BLOOMING" because of her."

~ Elder Tannie Hill

BLOOMING INTO YOUR PURPOSE: BREAKING THROUGH

"I am extremely grateful that God allowed my path to cross with La Deema Burns. Through a mutual friend, she and I were connected and have remained friends ever since. Her faith and iBloom Ministry have been inspirational. Always having a kind word to say, La Deema has remained consistent in spreading God's love. She had me on as a guest of her *phenomenal* radio show, and I am very grateful for the opportunity to shed light on domestic violence while being a beacon of hope for both victims and survivors. God has blessed her with a **powerful** platform that has allowed people to take off the mask of being ashamed and begin the healing process. Overall, La Deema has an *extraordinary* testimony that provides hope to the hopeless. She is a Kingdom Builder and servant of the Most High!"

With Sincere Gratitude,
~ *Jennifer C. Foxworthy*, CEO of Inspirationally Speaking, LLC

"I met La Deema Burns three years ago through social media. God used her to uplift and encourage me when I needed it the most. In 2015, I was granted the privilege of meeting La Deema at a Tea Party event where she was one of the guest speakers. I counted it all joy to finally meet the woman of God who had touched my life so much by her book, her godly wisdom, and her meek spirit. God is using her to reach many for His kingdom purposes."

Love you, my Sister-in-Christ.
~ *Kathy Haynie*

BLOOMING INTO YOUR PURPOSE: BREAKING THROUGH

"La Deema Burns has the anointing of Joseph. She has great vision, a keen business-sense, and the foresight and wisdom to launch others into their greatness. La Deema has been a catalyst for many artists, authors, and all those who are willing to put action to their faith. God uses her to open doors, enlarge territories, and ultimately to increase spheres of influence. She is a woman of God who has bloomed into her season. If you allow her to, La Deema will help you bloom into yours!"

~ *Lady A*

"God will create beauty from the ashes of your past!"

"La Deema is a witness to the healing hand of God. What a joy it has been to watch God at work in her life the past few years! I have watched her grow in her anointing and seen her use that anointing for the Lord's work. She is sensitive to the Spirit's move, and that sensitivity has opened the door for many to find healing in Jesus' name. From her first book, *Beauty for Ashes*, to this current book, *Blooming Into Your Purpose*...from her personal testimony to her iBloom Ministry...from her calling to her family – La Deema is a woman who wants God to be at work in **every** area of her life. I know that this book will be a blessing to every woman who turns the pages. The Spirit of God has anointed this project. Allow that *same* Spirit to apply this word to your life."

~ *Rev. Aaron Gross*, Logansport Church of the Brethren

Dedication

This book and the others to follow in the *Blooming Into Your Purpose* series are dedicated to each of you who need to know God has more for you. Know that you are not alone. God has a plan just for YOU from the beginning to the end and from the end to the beginning. No matter where you are in life, you can and will make it through the process of birthing your divine purpose.

God has called you to BLOOM into His divine purpose and plan He has for your life. It's time to come out of the ashes of your past pains, hurts, struggles, and trials. It's time to rise up and be the beautiful flower He has created you to be. This very day, receive His Crown of Beauty that was reserved just for you for such a time as this.

The word of the Lord is saying, "Trust Me, for I am your God. I will give you a better life. I am making a way for you. Many will be healed and delivered through the power of your testimony. Do not draw back; instead, blossom. Stand tall and strong, for I am your Lord God. I am with you. I have created you to be My people."

Trust in the Lord with all of your heart and lean not unto your own understanding. Allow Him to take the ashes and brokenness of your life and mold you into His masterpiece.

Acknowledgments

First and foremost, I want to thank God for birthing this project in and through me. I praise Him for this book and give Him praise in advance for the others that are to come.

To Co-Authors Darlene Duckett, Karen Perkins, and Kim Erwin: I thank God for your contributions to this project. I am grateful as well for the co-authors on future *Blooming Into Your Purpose* projects. I can't thank each of you enough for allowing God to speak to and direct you to come be a part of this life-changing assignment. Thank you for sharing your powerful life stories. I love each of you and truly appreciate you turning the odds in the favor of others whose lives will be greatly enriched by your testimonies. May God continue to use and bless you to help others overcome their trials and struggles.

To Cris Meadows: Thank you for being a part of my life, mentoring me, and pouring into my life in so many ways. I thank God for you, my Sister. I thank you for the partnership as we help each other fulfill God's divine purpose and plan for the lives He places before us. We will continue to enrich the lives of the young girls God sends to us as we help them be all God needs them to be. Thank you for being a part of this book and sowing into the many lives who will read it.

BLOOMING INTO YOUR PURPOSE: BREAKING THROUGH

To Pastor Aaron Gross: Thank you for always being there to lead me in God's direction for my life and the lives He places before me. Thank you for empowering me to not give up and to press through. You continue to encourage me to know that God's will is faithful to them who seek Him. For pouring into the lives who will read this book and the many lives you touch in our community and throughout, thank you. I am so blessed and grateful that God placed you in my life. You are a true man of God who is so in love with our Lord and His people.

To Andrea Smith, Jennifer Foxworthy, Tannie Hill, Dr. Walter Sims, Priscilla Warren, and Kathy Hayne: I can't thank all of you enough for being a part of my life. You each have a special place in my heart. You were sent by God for His purpose and plan, and I thank you for sharing your love for Him with me. Thank you for allowing God to use you in my life to be the blessings that you are. There are no words to express everything each of you means to me. Without you, I couldn't do everything God has called me to do to impact the lives of people He places before me daily. I praise God for you as we stand strong together, empowering each other to walk in our purpose for the sake of building the Kingdom of God. Thank you for your love and compassion. For that, I am forever grateful.

To my husband, Patrick: I thank you for always showing me so much love and support and for believing in me. You are my helpmate and my soulmate. Much like God, you never find fault in me. You build me up to be the wife, mother, and woman I am today. I love you, Patrick, for being YOU!

BLOOMING INTO YOUR PURPOSE: BREAKING THROUGH

To both my children, Patrick Mitchell and Arieon: Thank you! You have made me proud to be your mother. Thank you, **Mitchell**, for always pushing me to do better. You remind me that if I can think it and dream it, it can and will happen. I thank you for your passion and drive to keep pushing me in all I am doing. I know by looking at you and the person you are today, I have been successful at parenting.

To my sweet gift and blessing, **Arieon**: God gave you to me to save my life. Your coming pulled me out of the ruins I was in. Through you, He used you to birth the vision not only for this book cover, but the past one as well. I am so blessed He gave me another chance to experience childbirth and to bond with my newborn baby the way a mother is supposed to. I look at who God is making you: a sweet, talented, and gifted young lady who has so much to offer the world. You brighten my days and give me so much happiness and laughter.

To my Publisher and Editor, Angela Edwards: A special, sweet thank you for everything you have done to bring this vision to life! You are so amazing! I can't praise and thank God enough for placing you in my life. I am so excited to be working with you – not only on this project, but others to come.

To the wonderful book cover designer: Thank you for working countless hours to harness my vision and bring it to life with perfection. I appreciate how you allowed me to push you to use all of your God-given gifts and talents.

To ALL of my sweet and beloved Brothers- and Sisters-in-Christ: Thank you! Let's BLOOM!

Foreword
By Cris Meadows

I absolutely *love* flowers. I never knew why…until now. It's not just because they are beautiful; it's because they **BLOOM**! I think it's amazing to watch a flower rise above the darkness and dirt to push upward towards its own authentic beauty. During a storm, I love to watch how *everything* can be damaged, but the flower stays in full bloom!

It is amazing how much like flowers we are. Just when we think we are being buried in the darkness of the dirt, we are really being planted.

I once was a seed – not fully developed, but just a *possibility* of what I could be. I was a woman with a mission that was possible, but I did not know what the mission was or that the possibilities were **endless**. I was a woman who was stressed beyond my coping skills. I am a mother of twins who nearly lost my life while giving birth. I was the wife of a husband who identified himself with his past, never looking ahead.

One of my twin sons was born physically-challenged. His left hand did not fully develop and I did not know what, why, or how it happened. I never asked God why, but I ***did*** blame myself. I thought maybe it was something I did…maybe it was my past catching up with me for all the wrong that I did.

BLOOMING INTO YOUR PURPOSE: BREAKING THROUGH

Just when I started to ponder over those things, the Holy Spirit spoke to me and reminded me of St. John the 9th Chapter: When a boy was born blind, the people gathered and said it must have been the fault of the mother or the father. Jesus said neither had sinned for that thing to happen. Jesus said, *"It is for My glory!"* That has always been my comforting peace when it comes to my son: It's for **Jesus'** glory.

I developed into a homicidal, fake personality while internalizing the seed of hopelessness because I identified myself through the opinion of others. I considered myself a statistic. I never listened to the voice on the inside because the voices on the outside seemed to speak the loudest. Why? *Because I allowed them to.* It never occurred to me that I could have a say in what happened to me. It never occurred to me that I could make a choice in how this thing called "life" played out. I prayed. I fasted. I spoke in tongues. Yet I still felt like a dead woman walking.

You see, a seed does not bloom until it dies. Just when you think you are being buried, you are really being planted. I was just right to be planted to **BLOOM** into my full purpose because everything on the inside of me had died. However, not one thing changed until I decided: *"Transformation begins with me."* I had to change how I saw myself by asking God to show me how **HE** sees me. I needed my mirror to reflect the person God created me to be!

BLOOMING INTO YOUR PURPOSE: BREAKING THROUGH

You must understand that the seed doesn't spring forth until it is in the germination process. That is the process that allows the seed to develop – after a period of dormancy. Such as it is with life, just when life has stood still, nothing is happening, and we think it is over, **that** is when you start the blooming process.

The process of **MY** "iBLOOM" did not start just because I prayed, fasted, shouted, and obeyed God. It started when I decided to let go! Let it go so **you** can grow! That is when I began to **BLOOM**!

I started my organization, *Harvest Girls International, Inc.*, out of letting go. I created the life I wanted to have and dedicated my life to the call to help other women create theirs, too! I did not know that I could create what it could look like for me to be successful, to be a leader of myself, and to speak my truth. God gave us creative power. "I AM" is your creative power. Use it. Embrace it. Live in it!

"I AM Powerful!"

"I AM Wonderful!"

"I AM Awesome!"

Using your creative power is speaking the possibilities of what is yet to be or what you are becoming!

BLOOMING INTO YOUR PURPOSE: BREAKING THROUGH

Whatever is calling you to become "I AM", believe it! Everything you need for your purpose is in the Earth – so you can call it forth! God will bring people into your life who will walk with you and help you at the appointed time. I love how God will bring awesome people together who have the same heart and love for women. I love how they serve a mighty God to do a great work together.

I met La Deema Burns through a Sister-in-Christ who brought us together. We *immediately* bonded. I believe that La Deema has started a **MOVEMENT** that will cause a shift in the universe: "iBloom". When she said "yes" to her passion, her purpose started to emerge. La Deema is truly a woman who has a heart to empower, impact, and equip women to walk into their greatness by removing their excuses and giving them a platform to take the path into their destiny.

La Deema did not give up when she was seeking to find her way to the purpose to which she had answered the call. She prayed, fasted, trusted, and believed that God would do exactly what He said He would do for her to empower women. Let's not leave out that she did the work! She did what was required to become excellent in her Movement. "iBloom" is the most *amazing* name and program I have heard in a long time. It speaks to the world!

I truly believe God put La Deema and I together and He is using us to transform lives and to cause others to **BLOOM**! She has already started making a major impact in the world today. I am honored to be a partner with her as together, we fulfill the mission we are both so passionate about.

BLOOMING INTO YOUR PURPOSE: BREAKING THROUGH

I see La Deema doing things that will change the way people collaborate with one another by focusing on what *everyone* has to offer that will empower her and the next!

"iBloom" speaks to every woman who desires to grow and become the authentic, beautiful, gifted, and talented woman God has called her to be and to become.

"iBloom" speaks to the seed in all of us – and the purpose of a seed is to produce…to **BLOOM!**

I am honored to be a part of this amazing Movement that is taking the country by storm! I believe the best is yet to come. I believe women will be transformed by the renewing of their minds.

Lastly, *"Success is what you live, how you live, and why you live."*

La Deema has taught me these three things:

"I Love…I Live…I Laugh" because ***"IBLOOM"!***

~ *Cris Meadows*, Founder/CEO
Harvest Girls International, Inc.

BLOOMING INTO YOUR PURPOSE: BREAKING THROUGH

Preface

After penning my first book, *Beauty for Ashes* (a book about my life and how God took the ashes from my past and transformed me into His beauty), the word of the Lord came to me and the birthing process quickly began. Six months after the book's completion, God spoke to me about delving deeper into "Beauty for Ashes" to clarify its meaning. I referred my search to The Messenger Bible. My search brought me to an image: a bouquet of roses. **Immediately**, God said, *"I am gathering My daughters together as a beautiful bouquet. Some will be just budding. Some will be just opening with a few petals. Some will be in full bloom. You will walk hand-in-hand, empowering one another; for what I have placed in each of your hands, you will encourage one another. Together, you can do so much more than standing alone."* He birthed His ministry page through my Facebook Fan Page. God went on to further directed me, *"It is to be called the iBloom Movement. I have* **BLOOMED** *you so you can* **BLOOM** *others and impact the lives I have placed before you for My kingdom. You will do a radio show. I will bring you partners. You will do book collaborations. You will go into the seven cities I am calling you to. While there, you will connect with nonprofit organizations and ministries. You will help them with what I have given them to do for the kingdom. You will feed my people either on Thanksgiving or Christmas. You will build scholarships for young women so they can further their education."*

That was back in October 2014. When God gives you a word, you take that word and birth it. You seek His face and ask the questions: **How, when, and who is to be a part of this process?**

BLOOMING INTO YOUR PURPOSE: BREAKING THROUGH

In January 2015, the iBloom Radio Show was birthed. In March 2015, God directed me to host a show called "Blooming into Your Purpose: How Your Pain Pushed You into Your Purpose". I put the call out to my social media following (at the time, there were approximately 37,000 individuals), to which over 20 women responded and joined the event. God sent me an **amazing** coach who has been in radio and television for over 20 years to teach and guide me along the way. During the show's series, the women shared their pains, how God turned those pains into their purpose, and how they are **now** walking tall and strong. They did it! They broke through the ashes of their past! So many lives – including my very own – were forever changed since being afforded the opportunity to share their stories on the iBloom Radio platform.

Throughout 2015, I hosted two other "Blooming into Your Purpose" events. God connected me with people in the seven cities He told me about previously. He was awakening His purpose in and through me. In Indianapolis, Indiana, He connected me with a wonderful woman by the name of Cris Meadows. She is the Founder of Harvest Girls International. Her organization empowers young girls from the ages of 9 to 17. Cris mentored and helped me so much with the vision God had given me.

BLOOMING INTO YOUR PURPOSE: BREAKING THROUGH

After doing the 2nd "Blooming into Your Purpose" event, there was a **major** shift in my spirit that had taken place. The new app, *Periscope*, was added to my vision. God instructed me to get connected, make even **more** Kingdom connections, and help others share what they are doing by inviting them to come on iBloom Radio. *Periscope* is where I met Dr. Walter Sims. His Scope is **The First Church of Periscope**. God spoke to me about Dr. Sims: *"Have him on the iBloom Radio Show."* Since Dr. Sims' appearance, others from Periscope have joined me on the show as well. **Another** shift in my spirit then occurred.

I heard the Lord say, *"It's time to unplug and sit with Me."* From September until December, I listened as God told me, *"It's time to reflect, rewrite, and revise how I am going to get you into the cities I have called you to. I'm now going to send you radio partners."* Dr. Sims was on the show in December. God spoke to me saying, *"He is your first partner. I have chosen him, and I will choose others."* As of January 2016, Dr. Sims became my first partner. God didn't stop there! At the time of this writing, I have a total of four partners.

BLOOMING INTO YOUR PURPOSE: BREAKING THROUGH

In February, God said, *"It's time for you to do the "Blooming into Your Purpose" radio event again. This time, I will limit the number of people you will have join."* At the time of this writing, 11 individuals joined and we are on the 9th show. God didn't stop there! After He gathered the 11, He then spoke to me about doing a book collaboration. Again, I put the word out before my social media following. Approximately 70 people wanted information on and inquired about how they can be a part of the project. God chose the women who are in this book and will choose those who are to be a part of the remaining books in the series. It was then God reminded me of a post from a dear friend about a Christian Book Publisher. He recommended I reach out to her. I did just that. This book is a result of that connection. Pearly Gates Publishing and I have partnered to help each other **BLOOM** into our God-given purposes.

See, you must **first** hear the word of the Lord. **Then**, you should write it down, meditate on it, and seek God's guidance as He takes you through the process. **Trust His process.** He may have to redirect your steps to get you to where **HE** needs you for His people. That is how God uses me. My purpose is to help God's people **BLOOM** by giving them a platform on which to share what God is doing in their lives, businesses, and ministries. I have been assigned to help them come out of the ashes of their pasts and **BLOOM** into who God has called them to be.

I have no doubt that when you read the stories in this book and the forthcoming ones in the *Blooming into Your Purpose* book series, you will see the **GLORY** of God! You will bear witness to His **DIVINE** healing power! You, too, will **BLOOM**!

Get ready to **GET YOUR BREAKTHROUGH AND BLOOM!**

Introduction

God has spoken: "It's time for YOUR breakthrough! Get ready to BLOOM!"

Blooming into Your Purpose is an assignment from God to bring His people together to share their stories of the trials, pains, and struggles they had to endure to birth the **purpose** to which He has called them. In *Breaking Through* and the remainder of the upcoming *Blooming into Your Purpose* series, the realness of everything the co-authors had to experience so they, too, could be used to help others **BLOOM** out of their past ashes and **BLOOM** into their purpose will be transparently shared.

God is calling His people to connect with me, La Deema Burns, as He uses me to help them **BLOOM** and reach an even wider audience through the different platforms He has birthed through me. From the social media following that is growing daily of over 80,000 individuals, to the iBloom Radio Show where there are *at least* five different countries and over 300 listeners tuning in regularly, the continual growth of my God-given ministries' blessings are evident.

Just as I did with my first book, *Beauty for Ashes*, within these pages, I share about my life and all of the brokenness I endured along the way. You see just a glimpse of where my life **was**, but more importantly, you see where I am **now** and how I am truly walking in my purpose.

BLOOMING INTO YOUR PURPOSE: BREAKING THROUGH

Darlene Duckett: God sent Darlene into my life as a guest on the iBloom Radio Show. She shared her story about how God is using her in the chapter, "God's Timing…Not Mine". She speaks of abuse, neglect, betrayal, teen pregnancy, and so much more. Today, she stands in faith and proclaims: **BUT GOD!**

Dr. Kim Erwin: Kim is a woman of God sent into my life specifically for this assignment. Her story will help her impact the lives God is placing before her through her story in the chapter, "The Blooming Bridge of Faith". She speaks of broken family ties, mistrust, and so much more – all the while assuring the reader that God remains faithful, loving, and is always our Protector.

Dr. Karen Perkins: Dr. Perkins is another individual specifically sent to me to be a part of this assignment as *Breaking Through* was being birthed. As an author, her newest book release, *Emotional Power*, hit the coveted #1 Best Seller spot on Amazon. Her chapter, "Find Your Happily Ever After Now – and Share it with Others", reminds us all of how much happier and fulfilled we will be when we choose an **Attitude of Gratitude** in **ALL** things. She writes, "Only then can we truly spread the message of hope and love with others."

Now is the God-appointed time to **BLOOM** again! The *Blooming into Your Purpose* series of books will enable others to write and share their stories to impact the lives of those who read them. Is God speaking to **YOU** and instructing you to write **YOUR** story? If so, feel free to reach out to me to be a part of this amazing life-changing project!

BLOOMING INTO YOUR PURPOSE: BREAKING THROUGH

A portion of proceeds from the sales of the series will go to feed families during the Thanksgiving and Christmas holidays, as well as build college scholarships for young women in the cities God has called me to.

Are you ready to **BLOOM**? Join us on this **AMAZING** journey and see how God lifts each of us out of the ashes and gives us a **Crown of Beauty**!

~ *La Deema Burns*, Collaborator

BLOOMING INTO YOUR PURPOSE: BREAKING THROUGH

Table of Contents

What Others Are Saying _____ vi

Dedication _____ ix

Acknowledgments _____ x

Foreword By Cris Meadows_____ xiii

Preface _____xviii

Introduction _____ xxii

BLOOMING Story by Darlene Bond

GOD'S TIMING...NOT MINE _____ 1

BLOOMING Story by La Deema Burns

The BLOOMING Process Isn't Easy _____ 9

BLOOMING Story by Dr. Kim Erwin

The BLOOMING *Bridge of Faith*_____ 29

BLOOMING Story by Dr. Karen Perkins

Find Your Happily Ever After Now – and Share It with Others _____ 43

Write YOUR own BLOOMING story! _____ 59

Authors' Biographies _____ 71

CONNECT WITH LA DEEMA BURNS_____ 75

BLOOMING INTO YOUR PURPOSE: BREAKING THROUGH

BLOOMING Story by Darlene Bond

GOD'S TIMING...NOT MINE

GOD'S TIMING...NOT MINE

What is MY Blooming Story? Early on in life, I faced many things I had no desire to experience. I have been mentally and physically abused…**BUT GOD!** I have been neglected, falsely accused, mistreated, betrayed, and an outcast…**BUT GOD!** I am a woman who had to learn about life all on my own…**BUT GOD!** I gave birth to my first child as a teen and was a high school dropout…**BUT GOD!** *(I returned to school a year later.)* No doubt, my life has been rough. Through it all, God has been my strength, joy, and hope. I learned to depend on Him during the storms of my life. I **knew** He made me for a *purpose*.

My children were raised in a single-parent household – *my own* – with **no** help financially or otherwise from their fathers. I made the sacrifice by working three jobs. I have been sleep-deprived on many an occasion – but I **never** gave up. I knew I wanted better for my children, so I always put their needs before my own. Currently, I work in the medical field as a Certified Nurse Assistant and Medical Assistant. In 2015, I became a Certified Life Coach. I have been tasked with helping others learn how to invest in themselves and discover their own God-given talents. As well, I teach them how to start businesses and the steps necessary to become a success.

BLOOMING INTO YOUR PURPOSE: BREAKING THROUGH

In 2010, God gave me a vision. In the vision, I saw babies and pregnant women. I didn't know what to make of it all. I started doing research and was able to make sense of the direction God was leading me towards. One of my first birthing missions was to establish a nonprofit organization that is now called *"God's Lovely Butterflies Maternity Home"*. My goal is to open a maternity home for teenage and single mothers. I envision housing them and their babies while providing GED, parenting, cooking, financial, job-readiness, and computer classes. Once the new mother leaves the maternity home, she will have the survival skills needed to care for themselves **and** their children. Each and every single day, I work towards my vision, although admittedly, it is challenging at times.

In the interim, I have dedicated my time and gifts to help those in need. One way I use my gifts to bless others is by hosting a Back to School Drive filled with school supplies for the less fortunate children in the community. That has been done for the past six years. Yet another way is through food boxes donated to the needy elderly every November. At Christmas time, Toy Drives are sponsored for the disadvantaged children to ensure they have a wonderful Christmas holiday. On a daily basis, my organization assists teenage and single mothers by providing them with the essentials for their children such as diapers, wipes, clothing, baby hygienic items, strollers, car seats, and formula. Most recently, the Facebook group entitled *"Help Me! I'm a Teenager or Single Mother"* was formed to give positive information to the mothers.

GOD'S TIMING...NOT MINE

In March of 2015, my mother passed away. She was the only parent I knew. A week before I was scheduled to meet my father for the first time, he passed away. Having to care for my mother was the hardest thing in life I ever had to do. I had to first forgive her for beating me at the age of eight and for not giving me the love I so desperately needed and desired as a child. Still, I set those ill feelings aside to care for her after her third stroke. That stroke caused major and irreparable damage. She couldn't walk nor talk. I was burdened with making major decisions concerning her care and her very life: Surgery or not? Let her live the remainder of her days in the state she was in? The doctors had given her two weeks to live – something I did not immediately tell my family. I prayed and prayed while hoping for the best. Mother's condition never improved, and watching her suffer daily was devastating. Three months after that stroke, she passed away. I bore witness to the end of her earthly life. I did not know then that the **one** day I chose to spend the night with her would be the last night I would have with her alive on this side of Heaven. Preparing for her funeral and burial showed a strength in me I didn't know existed. I am grateful to God I was able to make peace with her before her passing. I genuinely forgave her for all she had done **to** me and was thankful for all she did **for** me. As a parent, I realize *now* that it had to be hard on her raising twin daughters all alone without the help of their father...

BLOOMING INTO YOUR PURPOSE: BREAKING THROUGH

Life has its ups and downs. I have chosen to accept the challenge. God has not brought me this far to leave me. At the time of this writing, there is one major hurdle I have yet to overcome, but I know God wants me to trust Him. Currently, I am in school to become a Licensed Vocational Nurse. I am determined to beat the odds – after all, God makes **NO** mistakes. I am determined and dedicated to being the best I can be and be a walking testimony for Him. God did it for me, and He can do it for you. I am laying claim to *everything* God has for me. I will be the wonderful butterfly God has called me to be!

My second divorce took a lot from me. I lost my house, the contents therein, and **thousands** of dollars. My now-ex-husband also set me up to get felony charges of Terroristic Threats and Assault in an attempt to gain full custody of our seven-year-old. After fighting for almost three years for custody of my youngest daughter, the judge dismissed **both** charges – but not before the lawyer hired to represent me took my money and left me without representation, which left me to represent myself. After praying and doing extensive research, I became aware of the right things to say to get the court to grant things in my favor.

In 2016, God restored all that I had lost in 2013: my mind, my peace, my joy, my hope, and my love. He taught me that I can trust Him with the storms in my life. I learned He can do everything better than I can when I leave it all to Him.

GOD'S TIMING...NOT MINE

I have always desired to have a business that accomplishes multiple tasks all in one place. I stepped out on faith, took, and passed the insurance test. I can now sell Auto Insurance. As time progresses, I intend to add Life, Health, and Commercial Insurance to my repertoire.

In April, I married my Boaz – the man I prayed to God for who will love my children and me…the man who will **stay** by my side through it all. Scripture tells us that God gives us the desires of our hearts! God made sure I was equipped to handle everything He sent my way. When I give it all over to God, I don't panic or stress. How can I **not** trust Him?

It may take many years and a floodgate of tears to get what God has for **you**, but His Word *never* comes back void. I'm living proof that God can do **ALL** things – not just some. I know that without God, my life would be incomplete. You have to be willing to weather the storm. We can't rush God. He has His own timeframe to do His work in our lives. Always remember: Good things come to those who wait. I'm grateful that He chose me to be among His chosen. The gifts and talents He has blessed me with are used for **His** glory. Every storm sent my way, I weathered them. There were many tearful nights when I asked God *"Why me?"* – when I **should have** been professing, ***"Thank you, God, for choosing me to be a living testimony!"***

BLOOMING INTO YOUR PURPOSE: BREAKING THROUGH

I knew at an early age I wanted my children to have better than I had. I grew up in an apartment; my children are growing up in a house. I'm not on government assistance and work hard daily to accomplish all that I want in my life. My children won't have to depend on anyone because I'm building a foundation that will benefit them and their families to come. I have worked since the age of 15 and, in the process, learned great responsibility early on in life. Still, there are some things I wish I could have changed along the way.

I have set a goal that **will** be met: By the age of 40, I want to be able to work full-time for *myself* – not another establishment. I want my businesses to work for me. I want to be able to live comfortably and enjoy life. Presently, I am moving at a fast pace because I realize that life is short. I desire to bring to realization **everything** I have set forth to do. There are days I get frustrated when I think of all the things the devil sent my way to distract me. The strength I have has gotten me through this thing called life. I can't question God because He does things we may not understand. Imagine going through all that you do in life while holding on to God's promises through it all…

God showed me and now I *know*: It is in **His** timing…Not Mine.

BLOOMING INTO YOUR PURPOSE: BREAKING THROUGH

BLOOMING Story by La Deema Burns

The BLOOMING Process Isn't Easy

THE BLOOMING PROCESS ISN'T EASY

In 2012, God began to **BRIGHTLY** illuminate the path He would have me to take on this life's journey. My Spiritual Grandmother prophesied that He was birthing a ministry in me and that soon, **ALL** would be revealed. What started out as my being a saleswoman for a health and wellness business soon grew into something truly remarkable! It was through my obedience to God that I was able to financially bless other ministries and **BLOSSOM** into a ministry of my own.

God has called me to preach the gospel.

God has called me to break loose the shackles and set the captives free.

God has called me to help heal the brokenhearted.

God has called me to save my Brothers- and Sisters-in-Christ from bondage and brokenness.

God has called me to return to the place He removed me from to do those things and more.

THAT is where my story began...

My story begins – just as everyone else's does – in my mother's womb. The questions about my future were asked in accusatory tones: *What was the baby going to be like? Would she have all of her fingers and toes? Will she be normal? What birth defects are **SURE** to plague her? Will she be mentally retarded?* Valid questions...in light of the fact that my mother and father were cousins.

BLOOMING INTO YOUR PURPOSE: BREAKING THROUGH

As I became of age and began to learn of the relationship in which I was conceived, it was told to me that my grandmother shunned my father. There were stories told that my parents were made to sleep in the cold basement of my grandmother's house. The pressure from all sides was too much for my father and he left us when I was just a couple of months old. He moved to Alabama and started a new family there. *(My mother did the same. After giving birth to me and soon after my dad left, she became pregnant with my brother.)*

There my mother was – a single parent with two children at a time when a single-parent household was not commonplace. My maternal grandmother and my aunt (my mother's oldest sister) told my mother that Social Services was **sure** to take custody of either my brother or me if she didn't give one of us to my aunt. My mother, not having the means to care for both of us, gave my brother to my aunt to raise. After my aunt legally adopted him, he was raised as my cousin – *not* my brother. I always knew him as my brother, but I also knew not to mention as much because it would upset my aunt. I have always kept that secret close in my younger years.

When I was around two years old, my mother married my stepdad. To this day, he is the **only** man I have known to be my *father*. It didn't take away the sting from feeling abandoned and rejected by my biological father, though. Whenever I would inquire about him to my mother, she would remind me that *"he left us and started a new family"*.

THE BLOOMING PROCESS ISN'T EASY

At the age of four, the molestation began. My mom had a family friend who we called 'uncle' who used to stay with us. He was mildly retarded. While living with us, he provided my mother with money for some of the most basic of needs. On many occasion, he babysat my new baby brother and me while my parents went out on the weekends. *Oh. Yeah. My mother had a child by my stepdad.* I can recall the first time I was molested by "uncle". I was lying down on the couch with him and he made me fondle him. At four years old, I didn't understand what was going on, but I knew it didn't **feel** right. That same thing happened a couple of other times before I shared with my mom what he had done. I remember her getting *very* angry with him, threatening him with an iron skillet, and telling him to leave - he was no longer welcome in our home. Well, **THAT** didn't last for long. A couple of weeks later, he was back!

I clearly recall my mother saying to him, *"Well, you can stay, but you can't do **this** and you can't do **that**."* Shortly after his return, my mom again leaves me in his care. Guess what? Things became progressively **worse**. Instead of me touching him, he was touching me in inappropriate places and doing inappropriate things to me! I didn't feel as if I could even mention it to my mom. After all, she let him come back!

There was one time I can recall getting ready to take a bath. I was getting undressed and my mom asked me, *"Why do you have on so many pairs of underwear?"* While I don't remember my response, I do remember thinking, *"If I put on enough pairs of underwear, **he** can't touch me."*

BLOOMING INTO YOUR PURPOSE: BREAKING THROUGH

As I stated, my parents would go out on the weekends…drinking. They would come home and have arguments and fights. I was very frightened. My mom was very violent towards my dad most of the time. I felt she was the one antagonizing him and creating the arguments. I didn't know what to do. I didn't know what I **could** do. The adult parties in our home, the endless fighting, and the drug and alcohol use was too much for me to deal with. I ended up disassociating myself from the chaos.

Around age nine, I recall spending a week with my aunt. I loved spending time at her house because it was my place of escape. I can remember cooking meals for my two younger cousins and me because my aunt wasn't home to care for us. This one time, we were **very** hungry and the only thing available to eat was a package of hamburger in the refrigerator. *I must mention here that her house wasn't in the best condition. It was always kind of dirty: dirty dishes, clothes flung around, things not in their proper place. I would help where I could while I was there.* Anyway, back to the hamburger. I put it in a pan, cooked it on the stove, added some ketchup, and my cousins and me ate spoonful after spoonful until our little tummies were satisfied. *I later found out my aunt was a heroin addict. That's why we were left alone often.*

THE BLOOMING PROCESS ISN'T EASY

Then came the rape by one of my aunt's neighbor's children. The boy had to be about 12 years old to my nine. Against my protests for him to stop touching me, I was raped by him – and it was **painful**. When he was done with me, he pulled up his pants and simply walked out. I felt *sick*. I felt *dirty*. I felt *ashamed*. I felt *hurt*. I called my mom – because, again, my aunt wasn't anywhere around – and she said, *"Well, you'll be okay. Everything is going to be alright. I'll be there in a couple of days to get you. You're okay."* Not once did my mom ask where my aunt was. I was left feeling alone, rejected, and abandoned by my mom. Anger and resentment began to set in. I began to act out and do things to purposely get into trouble.

At the age of 13, I met a boy – well, a ***man*** – who was 19. He had come to my cousin's graduation party, was paying attention to me, and whispering sweet nothings in my ear. Not long after our meeting, we were in the basement having sex. This time, it was my choice. He didn't **force** himself on me at all. This was my mindset at the time: *Here is someone showing me much-needed attention. Could he possibly be the one to be there for me?* I wasn't making good choices at that time in my life. I was hurt and broken…looking for a rescuer. Soon after, he became my boyfriend. My father didn't approve of the relationship, but my mother did – which angered my father tremendously.

As time went on, I would prove my defiance by sneaking out of the house and not returning for a couple of days – just to spend time with my boyfriend. I wanted – no I **NEEDED** – to escape from home. I wanted to spend as much time with him as I could because he was scheduled to move back to Florida (his home state) at the end of the Summer. One of my first thoughts were: *I could go back with him!* I was **determined** to make that happen.

I ended up running away with him. He had a bus ticket to return, but neither of us had any money to buy a ticket for me. So, what did we do? We hitchhiked from Indiana! We slept in cornfields. We were picked up by a truck driver. In the midst of the trip, we were also picked up by the police in Ohio. My boyfriend went to the police station and I was placed in a temporary foster home until my mother came to pick me up. Needless to say, by the time my mother arrived, she was **heated**! As we were preparing to get back on the road, we passed my boyfriend sitting at a truck stop. I begged my mom to pick him up and take him back to Indiana with us – which she did.

After speaking with my boyfriend's mom, my mother agreed to let me move to Florida with him on the condition that his mother would enroll me in school *immediately*. I was ecstatic! I was getting away from the man who kept touching me and the mother who didn't care that he kept doing it!

THE BLOOMING PROCESS ISN'T EASY

*Sidebar: I eventually began using the molestation opportunities to get money, rides, cigarettes, and other things from "uncle". Yes. I will call it what it was: Prostitution and manipulation. If I was going to give him something of myself, then he was going to have to pay in **some** way.*

Well, we make it to Florida – just to learn that his home was just as dysfunctional as my own! His mother failed to tell my mom that she was scheduled to go to court because her husband – my boyfriend's father – was having an affair…and she ran over the lady with her car! To boot, my boyfriend had been in trouble and was sent away to go to treatment for that! The **last** thing on his mom's mind was enrolling me in school. I sensed trouble! His mom was sentenced to prison for the assault. My boyfriend snuck out of treatment. There was too much going on! His dad came to live in the house in his mom's absence and basically said (in so many words): I had to go back to Indiana. My boyfriend wasn't having that, so we ran away in the middle of the night. We ended up at his brother's house. **They** get into a fight, so we couldn't stay there. We found an abandoned house and squatted there for a few days before making our way to his friend's house.

While at his friend's house, my boyfriend forced me to have sex with him one night. As we were having sex, I noticed a man standing inside the doorway watching us. He was pleasuring himself while watching us. The next day, I came across pictures of naked people and pornographic movies. I felt defiled and gross. *What if that man took pictures or made a video of us?* It was time to **GO**!

BLOOMING INTO YOUR PURPOSE: BREAKING THROUGH

To move the story forward just a bit, my boyfriend got a job stocking shelves at night, and we were able to rent a house from that same friend. I soon began to notice how his demeanor would change. He would get an attitude and freak out over the tiniest of things. I would simply blow it off. I was not allowed outside. He kept the curtains drawn both day and night. He would provide the excuse that I was supposed to be in school and that he would get into trouble because he was of age. It made sense to me at the time, so I didn't question it.

My boyfriend's controlling nature soon reared its ugly head. For example, I had written a letter to my mom and placed it in the mailbox. He removed, opened, and read it. *The gist of the letter was that I was homesick and ready to return home.* He was immediately enraged – and that brought on the first of many physical assaults. He grabbed me, hit me a couple of times, and started choking me. Flashes of my parents and brother ran through my mind as I was on my way to dying at his hands. He suddenly let my neck go then pushed me into the bedroom. He forced me to get undressed while he waved a boxcutter at me. We started having sex and while in the act, he was saying, *"I'll cut you so bad where no one will want you. If you go back home, your family isn't going to be the same. I will come and kill you and your family."*

I, of course, later received the standard apology of an abuser. I, of course, was asked for forgiveness. I, of course, was begged not to leave. I stayed.

THE BLOOMING PROCESS ISN'T EASY

We ended up losing the house and living in the woods again. We camped out there and would go to his mom's house during the day to take showers. That was my breaking point. I had enough. He wouldn't let me out of his sight, so I had to figure out some way to get away from him. I had no doubt he was capable of killing me and leaving me in those woods never to be found – because no one knew we were even out there! Then it came to me: I told him I needed to go to the bathroom. He told me to walk down a path – within his eyesight. As soon as he turned his back, I took off running for dear life.

I ran to a neighbor's house who lived across from his mom. She was a police officer. She let me in and I told her **everything** that happened since my arrival to Florida. I begged her to help me get back home. I had one phone number committed to memory: my boyfriend's co-worker. We called him, and he and his wife agreed to let me come stay the night with them and then drop me off at the bus stop the next day. I was ready to leave Florida and head back to Indiana once and for all.

Later that night, while sleeping on the couch, I was awakened by a man with his hand over my mouth. He said, *"Shhh…don't say anything."*

It was my boyfriend.

BLOOMING INTO YOUR PURPOSE: BREAKING THROUGH

I thought, *"Oh no. I'm in big trouble. He's going to beat me. He's going to kill me."* Instinctively, I calmed him down and told him I had to go to the bathroom. In order to get to the bathroom, I had to go through his friend's bedroom. I immediately jumped on the bed in a total panic. **"He's out there! He knows I'm here! He's in the house!"** His co-worker confronted him and told him he had to leave. The following morning, I was taken to the bus stop – a small convenience store. A payphone was nearby, so I called my mom to update her.

While waiting for the bus, a police officer pulled up and started questioning me. *"What are you doing here? Where are you from?"* He ended up taking me to the police station so that he could verify my story. I was **very** concerned about missing my bus. After checking out my story with my mom, I was driven back to the bus stop. I made it onto the bus and made calls along the way to let my mom know I was getting closer and closer to home. During one of those calls, she informed me that my boyfriend had called and threatened to burn our house down. Once I finally made it back to Indiana, I was **terrified**. *Would he come and burn our house down in the middle of the night while we were sleeping?*

THE BLOOMING PROCESS ISN'T EASY

Life between my parents wasn't much better than my own failed relationship. **Both** of them were having affairs. My mother was having one with a man who lived in the town she worked in who she knew through her brother. My father was having an affair with a woman who lived in another state. Divorce had been mentioned. I told my dad that I wanted to go with him if he left the state. His response was, *"I'd love to take you with me, but you're not really mine and I don't think your mom will allow me to do that. I'm taking your brother and sister and going to Alabama."* My heart was ripped out of me. **He's going to leave me with a woman I don't even trust to protect me? Really?**

Moving my story forward some more.

My dad left and took my siblings with him. My mom ended up being with the man from the town she worked in. We moved to the community where I reside currently in Indiana. My cousins and I began to hang out a lot. They indulged in drugs and alcohol. I wasn't a fan of the stuff…until then. I needed to numb myself from my reality.

One night, my mom and I got into a big argument **AND** physical fight. I said *horrible* things to her and called her all sorts of bad names. She ran into the bathroom and tried to kill herself by overdosing on pills – but her boyfriend stopped her. I knew then I could no longer live there. I was done with my mom – and my mom was done with me. She took me to my uncle's house (my biological father's brother). *Did I fail to mention all of this happened when I was only 14 years old?*

BLOOMING INTO YOUR PURPOSE: BREAKING THROUGH

Sidebar: Through it all, I loved my mom – even though I was angry and bitter. She was the only one I had – whether good or bad – who was there for me. She was my mom. We only get one.

Although my uncle was very strict, I was glad to be away from my mom. Not only was he strict; he was a binge drinker. He would drink constantly for **months** without eating – then pass out, get up, and start the vicious cycle over again. When I first moved in, he was going through one of those cycles. He and my aunt were having an argument about how their children should be disciplined. Suddenly, violence erupted and I thought: **HERE WE GO AGAIN!** In spite of that, I was *still* glad to be away from home.

My aunt was very loving towards me. She was a breath of fresh air after all I had been through. She catered to me because she had all boys and I was the only girl. For example, when my cousins went to the roller rink, she would come up with the money so I could go with them. When I was younger, we used to live across the street from them. She would baby me and take me places with her. I was like the daughter she never had.

What was unfortunate for everyone at the time when I stayed with them was that I was going through some serious changes. My uncle noticed – although I wasn't aware – that I was causing physical harm to myself while asleep. He once caught me standing in the middle of the living room sleepwalking with a pair of scissors in my hand. Apparently, I was making the motion like I was stabbing myself. He was very concerned and sought out professional help for me. I had a glimmer of hope!

THE BLOOMING PROCESS ISN'T EASY

When I visited the psychiatrist, we addressed many of the things I had bottled up inside of me that needed to be released. He put me on medication: an anti-depressant. I had **horrible** nightmares about my siblings being taken away from me while on that medication. I even gave myself a bloody nose one night in my sleep. Therapy continued and I was instructed to begin journaling my dreams so they could be discussed when I returned for my visits. Hope set in. I did not want to return home – ever. The drug abuse had stopped and I was beginning to feel much better about life.

My uncle brought much-needed structure to my life. I stayed with my uncle and aunt for the remainder of that school year and then with my best friend for the entirety of the Summer. While staying with my friend, I did things I shouldn't have been doing and hung out with people I shouldn't have been hanging with. You guessed it correctly if you thought, *"She started using again."* The medication administered by the psychiatrist had me feeling weird, so I stopped taking that altogether.

When I arrived back home (my mom's) at the end of the Summer, my parents' divorce was well on its way. There I was – back in the madness. My cousins and I started hanging out again, drinking and smoking. It began to hit me: *I didn't have **anyone** directing my steps and teaching me a better way to live.*

BLOOMING INTO YOUR PURPOSE: BREAKING THROUGH

I ended up getting into a couple of relationships that didn't work out. In one of them, even though the boy was my boyfriend, he raped me. Did I have a sign on my body that said, **"Here I am! Violate me!"?** Shortly after the rape, I was in a car accident and became addicted to prescription pills. It didn't take long for me to realize I had become an addict. I went into a 60-day treatment plan in an attempt to get my life on track.

Sidebar: *All throughout my life, I struggled with addictions and sexual traumas. From a young age, I thought to get what I wanted, I had to give myself away to make a man love and care about me. I couldn't have been more wrong.*

When I turned 19, I reached out to a good friend who would become my husband. He was very loving and compassionate. I didn't know how to deal with that, so I sabotaged our relationship by having an affair. Before that happened though, I became pregnant with our son. When I went to give birth, I became very sick. They put me on life support and into a medically-induced coma. They had to revive both our son and me three times each. All of this happened at a teaching hospital in Indianapolis. My medical condition was a mystery. They told my mom I had a 1% chance at recovery – and if I did recover, I was going to be a vegetable. God's miraculous healing of me on that hospital bed was the 2nd time He proved medical science wrong. The first time, I had an issue with my hip when I was born. The doctors said by the time I was 20, I would have severe arthritis and would be committed to a wheelchair. Before the age of four, God molded and shaped my hip. God healed me!

THE BLOOMING PROCESS ISN'T EASY

When I was in the coma, I saw who I believe was the devil and an angel fighting over me. Jesus came to me and showed me glimpses of Heaven and Hell. He proved to me that both were **very** real. I was instructed to share the news that both do, indeed, exist. You can believe the devil tried to tell me what I experienced never happened. He tried to tell me I was delusional because of the infection and the drugs the doctors administered.

My husband and I married a year after my son was born. I didn't want to marry him just because we had a child. I wanted to be sure he was the person I was to be with. I didn't want to have our son going through what I had been through with those feelings of abandonment and rejection – having parents going through a divorce and all of that other stuff that came along with what I knew marriage to be…but that's what happened anyway. We were married for almost seven years. He was, in my opinion, too good to be true. I was always waiting for the other shoe to drop. As I stated earlier, I had an affair. As soon as it happened, I immediately knew what I did was wrong. *What did I just do? Why did I just do that?* I told my husband what I did and we tried to reconcile. I became impatient with the process and didn't allow him time to heal. In a word, I was being selfish. We divorced.

Looking back, I believe God allowed us to separate so that we could each face our brokenness and seek Him as our Lord and Savior.

BLOOMING INTO YOUR PURPOSE: BREAKING THROUGH

A year or so after our divorce, I got into another relationship that was very toxic – fighting, drugs, and alcohol were the norm. I later learned that **he** was doing cocaine and meth. We were on again, off again. *By this time, my son was eight years old. I tried my best to shelter him from all that was going on, but children know more than we often give them credit for.* I once made a trip to a bar and had sex with a friend of my stepdad. I used protection but soon found out I was pregnant. I didn't know whose baby it was, so I told both my boyfriend and my stepdad's friend – although all signs pointed to my boyfriend as the father.

While pregnant with my daughter, I had finally reached my bottom. I could not live the life I was living any longer. I cried out to Jesus to come into my life and save me. As Christ always does for those who call on His name, He came and told me as long as I keep my focus on Him, He would restore everything back to me. I got on fire for God! I started going to church with my biological father. Then, my ex-husband and me became friends again. He saw a change in me and asked about it. I told him I was going to church and that my life had changed; I wasn't the same. He came to church with me and when he did, God stirred his heart to dedicate his life to the Lord. The Lord began to restore our relationship and marriage. Within a couple of months and after some counseling with the pastor, we remarried. At the time of this writing, we have been remarried for 15 years.

THE BLOOMING PROCESS ISN'T EASY

These past years haven't been without their struggles with my walk with the Lord, but God never stopped doing a greater work in me. Every time I would find myself faltering, I would come right back up. It was like being stuck out in the water with no life preserver. When the preserver came, I was safe…until I got tired and would slip through the hole…then the preserver would come for me again.

I had to ask God, *"How can one person go through so much and survive?"* I now realize I **had** to go through it all in order to save those God assigns to me. It's not about me; it's His divine purpose for my life. I stood in the fiery furnace and came out unscathed because Jesus was there with me. I didn't even have the scent of smoke on me.

God called me to speak. God called me to write. In spite of my difficulties – one of them being I was a high school dropout – God is using me. I stand on faith. He called me to it; He will help me through it. Today, I am helping others tap into their purpose. He called me to breathe life into others and encourage them to step into their purpose. I'm a Spiritual Life Coach, a Radio Host and Producer, an Author, and the Founder of iBloom Movement.

I recall God's revelation of iBloom. He said, *"I'm gathering my daughters as a beautiful bouquet of roses. Some will be buds. Some will just be opening. Some will be in full bloom. You're to walk hand-in-hand encouraging and empowering one another, as I have placed that purpose in your hand."* He went on to say, *"I bloomed you to bloom others. I bloomed you to walk alongside others."*

BLOOMING INTO YOUR PURPOSE: BREAKING THROUGH

In 2015, God began speaking to me about a radio show. I thought He was being funny. I am one who sometimes gets discombobulated with my words and pronunciations – but I trusted Him. He sent me a beautiful coach who had been in TV and radio for 20 years. When God calls you to it, He will equip you for it. You must be obedient and faithful – and just do it.

The radio show launched on January 26, 2015. I was a participant in an event: *24 Hours of Power*. There was over 40 women involved in the teleconference. My topic was 'Coming Out of Your Comfort Zone'. On the night I spoke, God had stirred in my heart to become a Spiritual Life Coach. I had been mentoring and coaching people for a few years, but I viewed it as ministry. God called me to empower and give others hope on a more professional level. He called me to help them rise up out of the ashes.

In March 2015, *Blooming into Your Purpose* was birthed. Over 20 women came on the radio and shared their stories of how they bloomed into their purpose – how their pain pushed them into their purpose.

This is how God oftentimes works: He will give you a seed by dropping a word in your spirit. We are to take that word, meditate on it, and set it before the Lord while asking Him for the fullness of the vision. As for me, I am a visionary. I see the things God reveals to me, but not the fine print. I wait on Him to give me full instruction. Too often, we get in a big rush because we're excited. That's why God can't reveal all the fine details that He's doing in our lives all at once. We wouldn't be able to contain it!

THE BLOOMING PROCESS ISN'T EASY

In March 2016, Blooming into Your Purpose has again gathered **phenomenal** women of God in this book collaboration that will grow into a series. God is going to do great things through the women who have and will join the series. I desire to speak directly to those women: There's more inside of you that needs to come out. This book is to encourage you to step out on faith and share even more of what God has done for and through you with your own book.

There are presently over 70,000 people who follow me all throughout social media. God is using me as a bridge to connect people. I've been assigned to help them be seen and get a much farther reach. These past four years have been amazing! This is the season for God's people to bloom into their divine purpose. If more people in the body of Christ would step into their rightful place and take authority, we wouldn't have all the chaos we do in the world today.

As for me, where am I going? I'm going **up**! I'm going **greater**! God is going to keep enlarging my territory and the territories of those He places in my life. I believe God divinely connects His people together to advance the kingdom of God. It's not about me. It's not about you. It's about His kingdom. A very high price was paid for our lives. Jesus Christ paid for our lives on the cross. We need to do everything we can to be servants for God in this earthly realm.

Step into your purpose and be who Jesus needs you to be: the very image of Christ.

As I often say:
"GET READY TO BLOOM!"

BLOOMING INTO YOUR PURPOSE: BREAKING THROUGH

BLOOMING Story by Dr. Kim Erwin

The BLOOMING *Bridge of Faith*

THE BLOOMING BRIDGE OF FAITH

Memories came crashing over me as if it were yesterday…although it was 22 years ago. At the time, I was sitting in mediation with my daughter as she battled visitation with her son's father. Our mediator was a fledgling attorney I hired all those years ago to regain custody of my **own** daughter.

The pain was deeply etched in my heart and soul as I remember coming home from work at noon to find a lone teddy bear sitting in the middle of my daughter's bedroom. **Everything** else was **gone**! My erratic heartbeat's pounding was immense. In the moment, it was all I could hear. The flood of questions came. *Where is she? Where is my husband? My mother-in-law had moved in with us and she was gone, too. His two children from a previous marriage: gone. What is going on?* I had no answers to those questions and a dark veil of confusion, disbelief, and dread filled my whole being. As the fog lifted, I returned to work and tried to locate my family. It became apparent after a few hours of searching that my husband took everyone and hired movers to relocate our daughter and his family to an undisclosed location. I prayed to God with a desperate plea: **Please, God: Help me!** I knew that God would never give me more than I can handle.

BLOOMING INTO YOUR PURPOSE: BREAKING THROUGH

When I checked our joint checking account, **all** the money – *just like my husband and daughter* – was gone. When I attempted to fill up my car with gas, the credit card didn't work. I soon learned all of my credit cards were cancelled. When I returned home that day, the automatic garage door opener wasn't working. It turned out all of the utilities were cut off. Gazing throughout the house, I realized I had just purchased groceries the day before, so I returned the perishable foods. The cashier must have seen the agony and despair on my face because **no** questions were asked. I was able to fill up my car and food had lost its appeal.

Thank God, my brokerage company advanced me money on my commission and the school where I taught Real Estate classes advanced me as well. The young attorney I hired was going up against one of the toughest attorneys in the city and state. There seemed to be no hope at all. My daughter was my life and I would see the fight through until the very end. We had only *days* to prepare to go before the judge.

As I replayed the conversation of my life story in my mind, I wondered where I got lost. *Why did I allow someone to use and abuse me?* Certainly, that was not the purpose **God** intended for me. I began to doubt my faith.

It was in those darkest hours when I began to be shaped and defined into who I was to become.

Realization set in that my family's disappearance was neither an accident nor coincidence. It had been planned out very well for quite some time. I also realized it was not really about me, but rather an indication of how my husband felt about himself.

THE BLOOMING BRIDGE OF FAITH

The early morning rays of sunlight greeted a sleepless night. I wondered how my daughter was doing. I knew that I needed to get to the attorney's office, but my heavy heart felt like a bulldozer stuck in the mud. My inner-voice reminded me that the kindness I had shown was mistaken for a weakness. The best character trait I possessed was stomped into the ground while the essence of me was stripped to the bone. As the ashes slowly settled around and covered me, it was then I realized: *I would come through this much stronger with an unshakable faith in God!*

As I poured out my life story to the young attorney, he wrote down **everything** and kept diligent notes. I thought to myself, *"Am I the only one to experience this or have others gone through similar ordeals? Am I a bad person and simply didn't realize it? No one has ever treated me like this before."* It was hard to shelve those thoughts, but I knew I had to. Getting my daughter back was the most important task at hand. My attorney stated the odds were stacked against me and that it would be a very hard battle. The plan to take my daughter away had been carefully planned and executed. Nonetheless, he said he would give my case priority and help me along the way. All I could do was trust him and hope he would be able to navigate through the deep, dark pit of adversity.

The next challenge was to tell my grandparents what happened. They had just moved to be closer to me and spend their last few years enjoying life. I will never forget the devastating look my Nana gave me. The questions came…I had no answers. She held me and instructed me to pray because prayers were the keys to open the heart of God. When I left their house, I learned my husband stopped by my grandparent's home – with my daughter in tow – to talk to them, but he told them they couldn't hold her. *They later told me the hurt they felt was one of the worst they had experienced in their entire lifetimes.* My Nana's sister passed shortly after that visit. Grief was everywhere and so overbearing, I couldn't breathe. **Wouldn't it be easier to jump off a bridge?**

It certainly wasn't in God's plans. The emergency hearing was set. My mother and aunt flew down to be with me. As I walked into the courtroom, each step felt like a hundred weighted steps. I was filled with so many emotions in such a short amount of time. We were called before the judge and as the judge read my response, he looked at me and said, *"You will get your daughter back."* The innocent side of me was looking for the best in the misunderstanding of family and trust. Joy and elation filled my soul! I thought it was over. I was totally wrong.

THE BLOOMING BRIDGE OF FAITH

My husband, daughter, and extended family disappeared **again** without a trace less than a week before the formal hearing. The devastation I felt is so hard to put into words. I wondered: *Did they leave the country? Did he kill himself or my daughter?* I prayed harder and harder and promised the world to God if He would just help me. The burden was getting greater and heavier…and I was growing weaker. That night, I dreamt my daughter was in my arms and that God said He would never leave me. When I awoke, I realized there was **no quitting** on my part. I needed to dig deeper trenches and always keep my guard up. *Why did I think I could fix people and make them better?* That job was designed **exclusively** for God to accomplish. I gathered my scattered seeds of faith and planted them deep. They needed tending to in order to produce a much larger harvest later. That was *one* large turning point in my life.

The night before the court date, I found out my daughter and husband's family were staying at my condo on the beach. My husband's first wife flew down to help me out at court. *I am forever grateful for her act of kindness.* She and I approached the door to the condo and knocked. He came running out of the door and into the parking lot with my daughter in his arms screaming some of the most **horrible** things ever. That was a side of him I had never seen so explicitly before. Defeated *(for the moment)*, she and I returned to my home and prepared for the next morning. It was unnerving listening to the tick-tock of the clock. It felt like a hammer was being pounded on my heart…

BLOOMING INTO YOUR PURPOSE: BREAKING THROUGH

The courtroom can be such a cold and unfeeling place - one where you have everything to prove…even *false* allegations. As I listened to the cases being presented before my own, I wondered how people can live like that. Character and integrity seemed nonexistent. A consensual downtrodden feeling of helplessness compounded over time filled the room. I know court is designed to protect the innocent and puts the burden of proof on proving innocence, but how do **families** fall through the cracks of society?

My turn before the judge came.

As my young attorney presented my life story, my mother heard firsthand about the beginnings of my marriage. One time, my mobile phone was used to beat the top of my head until the blood rolled down my face. My attorney recounted all of the cheating, drinking, and drugs my husband indulged in that I hid from everyone. My mother cried. *Afterwards, his attorney stated he hadn't heard so much character assassination in all of his life. The judge told him that maybe he should have interviewed his client better.* In addition, the judge told my husband that if my daughter was not delivered to my house by a certain time, he was to be called **directly**. My mother quickly requested the judge's number. My daughter was soon returned to me.

THE BLOOMING BRIDGE OF FAITH

I relished **everything** my daughter said and the beautiful schoolwork I displayed prominently on my refrigerator. There was no way I could ever live without her. My grandparents loved her so much, but I began to truly take notice of how much more they were aging. My sweet Nana gave me some of the best advice ever: **God is always first, family is second, and the rest is last.** Those were the *wisest* words I ever heard and are etched permanently in my heart and soul.

Some of the wisest and most loving people fly into our lives for a short time, but their impact lasts a lifetime.

I thought my problems were over, but they instead got worse.

The tricks didn't stop. The grew increasingly more outrageous. One evening, after midnight, the doorbell rang. I went to the door with my daughter at my side – and then the phone rang. At my door were two men with police badges asking for me to open the door. I stopped to answer the phone and my husband told me not to let the men in, but I had already opened the door. The smell of alcohol permeating from them was so strong. I somehow found the strength to push the door shut and lock it. I heard one of the men say, *"I didn't know her daughter was with her!"* Apparently, the men were sent to my house after a night of drinking with my husband…who guaranteed them a **"good time"**.

I went to the police the next day and was promptly told that it was a civil matter. My thoughts were, *"What if I was raped and killed with my daughter there? What would they do to her?"* It hit me like a ton of bricks: **That's** how so many women are killed. It is a civil matter until a rape or murder is committed – and then it's too late for the victim. There is such a fine line with the law…one I knew nothing about.

As the case moved forward, my husband tried to commit suicide…*twice*. The guilt I felt was insurmountable. *Why me? Why?* Every day was such a challenge and I knew my daughter would be affected by the craziness around her. The divorce **needed** to be granted so everyone could move on with their lives.

When my Nana died, so did a piece of my heart. My most positive force who told me I could be anything I wanted or do anything once I set my mind to it had left me. My corner was empty – until my chameleon husband came back **promising** to be a better husband and father. In my weakness and vulnerable state, I believed him.

We flew back home on Christmas Day to bury my Nana. It was painful, but at the same time, it looked like my family **would** be able to pull together. While at the airport waiting for our return flight, my husband whispered in my ear, *"Your Nana would turn over in her grave if she knew what a whore you are."* I was paralyzed with fear, knowing that it was going to get bad quickly. I had **no** family close to me. Fear became my reality.

THE BLOOMING BRIDGE OF FAITH

I eventually built up the courage and money to hire a divorce attorney who got the job done. The divorce was divided up into segments, with custody being my number one priority. The next phase was comprised of our combined business venture. The judge awarded it to me and I divided it up. The fight didn't stop, though. It lingered on for years and years. The next hurdle was that my husband didn't pay the IRS and his child support was delinquent. He told the IRS that he would give his one-half interest in the building to them to auction off.

My prayers never stopped. As a matter-of-fact, they *increased*. My faith was strong and I sought God's direction. At the time, I was prepared to shut down my business – but I knew I couldn't move home because I would have to leave my daughter. The only viable option was to negotiate with my husband. I told him I would forgive the past, present, and future child support, pay off his IRS debt, and he could deed his interest over to me. The only caveat was there could be no additional debt incurred. The child support from his first wife showed up, and I paid that off as well. She and her children certainly deserved it.

He opened an office 50 feet from mine and would constantly pick up clients and customers from my parking lot. He would tell people that I was out of business. He even told others that I had *died*. The list of evils grew longer day-by-day and year-by-year. One day, I woke up and realized it would never get better on its own.

BLOOMING INTO YOUR PURPOSE: BREAKING THROUGH

That was the defining point in my life. I shook off the ashes and raised myself up to live the life God had designed for me. There was a purpose He had in mind for me to go through what I had. I realized God had always been there. He carried me in my darkest hours until I could stand on my own. He stood with me in all the battles. *Maybe there's **someone** who could benefit from the sharing of my experiences!* Once my purpose came to light, it became my beacon in the darkness…my North Star in my compass of life.

In my business, I see the hurt, frustration, lack of hope, and desolation the people experience in every situation. I let them know they aren't alone and that I will help them over the threshold of life and on to their next chapter. It is in those defining moments when I realize God wants us to help others as He helps us. **Everyone** has a story and a defining moment, but not everyone has someone to help them. Almost everyone is at a different point in life when they face gut-wrenching, life-changing experiences. It is our reactions to those actions that define us and chart our course. I suddenly realized that I didn't recognize my value and self-worth. It took others' stories to make me realize my own.

THE BLOOMING BRIDGE OF FAITH

Soft whispers were murmuring in my heart and soul. **It was time!** The time had come to acknowledge my value and worth. I searched for my purpose as if it were a life mission. Then, those self-depreciating thoughts came to mind that maybe I wasn't worthy enough to help others. Countless heartaches and disappointments had discouraged my soul and troubled my heart. Oh, those whispers were getting louder… I started feeling ***boldly*** brave. I was **sure** there were other injured souls I could help and add value to.

When reality hit me, I knew those bad past experiences were a sum of my whole life. Joy gurgled and bubbled up with a euphoric feeling of oneness with myself…*finally*! It was time to accept who I was and what I had been through. Those fleeting feelings of peace, hope, and harmony became stronger – like the beat of my heart. It felt like the gentleness of the hummingbird in search of the nectar…the elixir of life. My purpose became clear because I now know my self-worth. Thoughts and feelings started crashing all around me like a grand symphony of life. I am not dead, but rather reborn with a new purpose to fulfill. I wondered: *How many have hurt as deeply as I have? Could I help just **one**?*

My calling in life is so much bigger than me. The sum of my life's experiences is who I am today. I want to offer that sliver of hope and encouragement that would truly make a difference in others' lives. It just might be what tips the scale in someone's situation. So much *value* is often added.

BLOOMING INTO YOUR PURPOSE: BREAKING THROUGH

Back to the beginning of my story… I look at my daughter battling for her son – my grandson. She is **so** strong, concise, and knows what to do. I sit and watch her. The mediator – that formerly-young attorney from so many years ago – looks at my daughter with respect and admiration. Life truly comes full circle.

My daughter, who almost lost her life in a bad car accident before Christmas, is here…in the present…and has grown into the **finest** woman and mother I have *ever* met. She walks with a limp, but she has her legs. A car can be replaced; a person can't. It is her specialness that helps so many people. She is strong inside…so much stronger than I ever was. That is what makes her uniquely her.

Forgiveness is a word that is easily said but not put into practice enough. I had a conversation with my now-ex-husband with my parents present a few years ago on an Easter weekend. He looked directly into my face, so I knew he was speaking from his heart. He explained that he doesn't have much recollection of all that he did because he was so messed up. Some of the stories were recounted to him. He stood up, apologized to my parents and me, and then looked at my daughter and said he was sorry.

It took so much to relive this story, but it is time to scatter the ashes to the four winds. Since doing so, I haven't looked back!

THE BLOOMING BRIDGE OF FAITH

Who would I be without my story? I don't worry about that because my story made **me** who I am today and shaped my daughter into the fine woman **she** is. Sometimes, our darkest hour defines who we are in the light. There was a time when there seemed to be no hope at all, but I chose to hang on for just a little while longer…the moment when one more breath seemed like a waste – but it really wasn't.

Each of us knows that special defining moment that changes **everything**. God's plan is ***BLOOMING***, after all. Faith is the bridge that gets us there.

BLOOMING INTO YOUR PURPOSE: BREAKING THROUGH

BLOOMING Story by Dr. Karen Perkins

Find Your Happily Ever After Now – and Share It with Others

FIND YOUR HAPPILY EVER AFTER NOW...

Time is precious.

Funny thing about time: I've found when I have enough time, others are often too busy for me. I've also found that I've far too often allowed myself to be too busy to give the right amount of time and attention to those around me.

Society once told us, "Serve first and then worry about yourself". Then it was, "Take care of you so there's more of you to give."

So, which is it? 'Lose yourself in service to others' or 'Focus on your own personal needs'? My answer? **YES!**

Again, time is precious. We don't have time to waste with things that harm or even destroy our happiness and the happiness of those we choose to surround ourselves with. One simple way to take care of ourselves and to serve others *simultaneously* is to develop a grateful heart while allowing joy and love to spill over to others. Develop hope, faith, and love – and share what you've learned. You see, it's not one or the other that we take care of. **It's both.**

Cornerstones of Attracting Your Happily Ever After Now are:

- ➢ Choosing to have a grateful heart.
- ➢ Developing a **true** attitude of gratitude.
- ➢ Having and showing empathy for yourself and your needs.
- ➢ Displaying empathy and awareness of the needs of others.

BLOOMING INTO YOUR PURPOSE: BREAKING THROUGH

Every once in a while, events take place that shape the person we are choosing to become. There are always options for our actions and reactions. Choosing wisely when the time comes stems from the practice of choosing wisely weekly, daily, hourly, **and** minute by minute. Your choice must be *preplanned*, *pre-resolved*, and *premeditated*. You've already made the decision; now you must practice until the choice is so infinitely right for a positive outcome that now or down the road, you no longer have to make a conscious decision.

The *choice* is **automatic**. The *choice* is **ingrained**. The *choice* is **natural**.

Through constant practice, we've already made the choice – one that will reveal the unique and wonderful people we are: People who bring joy and happiness to ourselves and others. We act...we no longer react. We simply do what we already know in order to create a true and positive outcome. This practiced state of mind is where Happily Ever After dwells.

You and I both know there are still times when we may go against our better selves. We can throw good judgment, good habits, and good attitudes to the wind.

FIND YOUR HAPPILY EVER AFTER NOW...

I'm no different. A few years ago, I had one of those days. You know the kind when you wake up grumpy and instead of choosing to determine the source of the emotion and do something about it, you go with the flow? Well, I decided to hold my own self-serving pity-party. Now, I say *self-serving* because that is **exactly** what pity-parties are! They provide nothing more than negative self-service that does **absolutely nothing** to improve you, the situation at hand, or your relationships with others.

On that particular day, I had chosen to feel sorry for myself. Yes. It was and is always a *choice*. I am going to say that **again** so that you may *choose* to receive it: **It is a choice!** It's always a choice! In that moment in my life, I had chosen the opposite of happiness, the opposite of gratitude, and the opposites of kindness, understanding, patience, and love.

So, there I was…creating one of those days when I was irritable from the time I woke up. Everything around me was annoying – and I just felt like being irritable. I didn't want anyone telling me not to be irritable, and I *certainly* did not want to think about gratitude towards anyone nor anything. Have you ever had one of those days?

That day, I told myself (if not consciously, subconsciously), *"You know what? Quite frankly, today is a terrible, horrible, no-good-for-nothing, very bad day. I don't want to be happy. I want to enjoy wallowing in my irritability."* I believe I was actually enjoying looking for all the horrible things around me just so I could prove it was a bad day.

BLOOMING INTO YOUR PURPOSE: BREAKING THROUGH

Let me take a moment to tell you a little about that terrible, horrible, no-good-for-nothing, very bad day. I had a speaking engagement in my hometown, which is *normally* a great thing. ***THAT*** day, it was irritating to me because my family was going to be away from home that evening. After the seminar, I had five long hours to sit alone at the airport before my plane took off to my *next* seminar.

Yes, I could have gone home…but then I would have been sitting home looking at the walls and doing nothing. As I said, **all** of my family had something else to do. On that day, I really felt like they didn't care enough to spend time with me. On top of that, I had to either pay for airport parking or for a cab to take me to the airport. So, I decided to go to the airport on the hotel shuttle. At least *then* I had a ***slight*** chance of catching an earlier flight – if there was one available **AND** if it was not already overbooked. I also justified being irritable because my flight was so late in the evening, it meant I would not get to my destination until the wee hours of the next morning.

Wow! Even I can tell how irritable and negative I was being!
Of course, with that attitude, some may say I was attracting negative events and energy. One might argue I *created* a negative spiral. Perhaps those things are true…perhaps not. What I can tell you is on **that** day, because I had chosen to be irritable, everything seemed to go sideways.

FIND YOUR HAPPILY EVER AFTER NOW...

When setting up the speaking room, **everything** went wrong. There weren't enough tables or chairs. The group that used the space the night before had spilled milk that had not been completely cleaned out of the carpet, so the room *reeked* of sour milk. The people who were supposed to set up and assist me with everything else didn't show up on time. The hotel couldn't find the boxes with the seminar materials. I mean, **COME ON! NOTHING WENT RIGHT!** Everything that could go wrong went wrong!

Since I teach and preach about having a good attitude, I was doing my best not to show how grumpy and irritable I was internally – all the while enjoying being miserable. I was trying to pretend on the *outside* that I wasn't having an awful, horrible, no-good-for-nothing, very bad day…but I was not having or allowing a **good** day! I was having a **BAD, BAD** day. I indulged in a completely selfish pity-party instead of displaying empathy for those around me. I **should** have acknowledged that which was not great, accepted it, and moved past it. I **should** have been looking for something around me that might be going *right*. I didn't. I instead chose to look only for the bad, the failures, and the misery.

That which we focus on expands. I chose unhappiness.

That day was challenging, but honestly speaking, I'd faced larger, more daunting challenges. As I faced greater challenges with a grateful attitude, things seemed to always fall into place. With a positive outlook, my mind was open to possibilities and creative solutions.

BLOOMING INTO YOUR PURPOSE: BREAKING THROUGH

That day, I could have chosen to problem-solve, but no: I was simply feeling sorry for myself. I could have clipped the feelings I had at the root. I could have – **I SHOULD HAVE** – said, *"I'm entitled to my feelings"*, and allowed myself to feel and process my emotions. I could have even shelved and processed them later at a more appropriate time. Instead of hope, faith, or appreciation, I was wallowing in a *'woe is me'* day. While I knew that I had the **option** of feeling it and moving on by saying, *"Okay. This is not my ideal day"*, I instead chose to make my negativity and irritability the focal point of everything around me.

Again: *That which we focus on expands.*

My negative day had expanded because I had stopped looking for good and, instead, looked for all the negatives I could find. Worse yet, even though I **knew** better, I didn't even stop to realize that's what I was doing!

Well, that day seemed to drag on forever. One bad thing after another took place. There was even a spider *(EEK!)* in my water! I mean, come on: **How much worse could it get?**

About 15 minutes before the end of the seminar I was presenting – at a **very** pivotal teaching moment – someone from the hotel came rushing into the room and said, *"We have an emergency call for you."*

FIND YOUR HAPPILY EVER AFTER NOW...

Your first thought (like most) was probably, **"Oh no! What happened?"** The sad truth is this: I was in such a foul mood and having such a wonderful pity-party that **MY** first thought was **NOT**, *"Oh no! Something bad may have happened!"* Instead, it was, **"Somebody better be dead or dying – or I am going to kill them for interrupting my session!"**

I will **always** regret that hideous, horrible, and self-centered thought. To this day, the negativity that I spewed out in that moment haunts me…

Fortunately, no one died. Still, the emergency was equally as heart-wrenching. You see, that call was about my youngest son. He had attempted suicide and was being rushed to the Emergency Room (ER).

The moment those words hit me are frozen in time. I will never forget… The room became deafeningly silent, with only the loud tick, tick, tick, **TOCK** of the clock just above me. The wrench of spoiled milk hit my stomach like a baseball bat hitting a home run. My heart felt as if it would explode at any moment. Basically, my world came to a painfully, screeching halt.

BLOOMING INTO YOUR PURPOSE: BREAKING THROUGH

That earth-shattering news did not know how to process within my brain. Out of sheer preservation, my conscious mind let go and my subconscious mind took over. Thankfully, in that moment, my practiced and now-ingrained habits kicked in. Through the conscious practice of **choosing** to have a grateful heart, the practice of searching for and developing a **true** attitude of gratitude, and learning to have and show love and empathy for myself **and** others, I was able to begin to process and cope with the news.

One habit that was particularly 'saving' in that moment was the search for gratitude. From 16 years of practicing the task of coming up with and writing down ten gratitudes daily, my survival instincts kicked in. Out of that practice and survival training, I turned to an attitude of gratitude. Yes, my shocked mind – in a state of not knowing what else to do – instantly went there out of sheer instinct and habit.

The question remains: *Why didn't my mind go there when I was irritable?* The answer is simple: ***I didn't want it to.*** I would not allow myself to feel gratitude. I *wanted* to feel sorry for myself. I made the **choice** to wallow. I wasn't having any part of empathy for myself or for the people around me.

Whenever I tell this story, someone always asks, *"What on earth did you have to be grateful for at that moment?"* Honestly, not a whole lot. Yet, as my gratitude kicked in, I started to realize I had **many** things to be grateful for.

FIND YOUR HAPPILY EVER AFTER NOW...

Here are a few of those *"Gratitudes"*:

1. My son was not successful at his suicide attempt.
2. He was found and rushed to the ER.
3. The hospital he was rushed to is one of the top-rated with leading experts in dealing with those types of situations.
4. I was in my hometown and had five whole hours to spend with him at the hospital.
5. I have a best friend who had gone through a similar situation.
6. I am not grateful my friend had gone through the situation, but rather that I had the opportunity to learn from her what to expect.
7. I am grateful I have a best friend I can call and cry with.
8. I am grateful for my family and friends, and for the love and support I knew they would give my son and me.
9. I am grateful for my faith.
10. I am grateful that I learned from the experience.
11. I am grateful.

Okay. I have to admit: There were **many** things to be grateful for on that day. What if his attempt had been successful?

I believe my gratitudes from years of habit would have still kicked in. They may not have been as positive – *or as many* – but still, they would have been there.

Here are some that might have been:

- I would have been grateful he was no longer in emotional pain.
- I would have been grateful for my best friend I could call and cry with.
- I would have been grateful for family and friends, and for the love and support they would have given.
- I would have been grateful, grateful…***GRATEFUL***!

See, gratitudes removed **ME** from the focal point. They removed the *"Oh, woe is me!"* It wasn't about me! Looking for gratitudes and *honestly* developing an attitude of gratitude helped me move past anger at myself and past guilt for not knowing or realizing his pain. It allowed me to love and forgive myself for not knowing what was happening in his mind and heart that had brought him to that point. It allowed me the freedom to put my shock, pain, and grief aside so I could focus on what really mattered. I had the freedom to love and empathize with him completely and unconditionally. It allowed me to focus on the real situation at hand and on the real person who needed me to focus on him. It helped me to focus solely on my son and what he must have been going through.

FIND YOUR HAPPILY EVER AFTER NOW...

That attitude of gratitude coupled with empathy put me in a position of an emotional power I didn't realize I had. Neither did I understand how much I was displaying it until months later. On Mother's Day, about nine months after that day, I learned the impact of those practiced, positive choices and behaviors when my wonderful son – who became healthy and happy – wrote an *Ode to Mother.*

What he expressed in that Ode was that it was my ability to focus on him and what he was going through, and my ability to have empathy – *not pity* – for him that gave him the strength to hold on and carry forward, instead of descending deeper and deeper into the aftermath of his darkest hour. It was my ability to use my emotional power that gave him hope and strength. It was his seeing in my eyes the sincere focus on him (instead of my own internal grief) that helped him believe things could possibly improve in his life.

He didn't have to coddle me, apologize to me, worry about how I was reacting, or how I might react next. He didn't have to worry about how I was feeling, what I was going to think, or how I was going to judge him. Knowing those things gave him the strength to take care of himself. It was seeing those practiced, positive choices that gave him the ability to see possibility. That possibility led to hope – and that hope led to a flicker of courage. The smallest spark of courage allowed him the faith to use the tools I shared with him that night.

BLOOMING INTO YOUR PURPOSE: BREAKING THROUGH

One tool I shared is one I have used for myself for years. Sadly, it wasn't until that night that I suddenly realized I had never used it with him. If I had, we *might* not have been caught sitting in the hospital.

That night, while in the ER, he and I discussed the specific tool of gratitude which leads to hope. I told him, *"Every night for the next two weeks, I'm going to call you."* (I knew that once they took him to his room, they would not let me see him for several days.) I went on to say, *"Every night when we talk, I'd like you to give me a list of 10 things you are grateful for on that day."*

For his first several days, all he could come up with for his gratitudes were bodily functions – much like it was for me when I first started that practice. Then, that **amazing** young man slowly began to add things to his list.

He was given other tools as well – resources that opened his mind to possibilities and to the power and purpose of his life. It was that flicker of courage through his freshly-understood strength and the ability to see that there were options and possibilities that gave him a newfound strength to go forward. It was seeing that **each** moment is a *choice*. Yes, there may be times when he would need extra support, counseling, or maybe even medication. He had to be the one to choose when it was time to seek out that help – should that need arise.

FIND YOUR HAPPILY EVER AFTER NOW...

You **MUST** allow positive to happen! Have empathy for yourself and others in their various stages of life. Don't look for annoyances. *There are way too many if you look.* Instead, search for and acknowledge love, kindness, and patience. Remove yourself from situations or people who would harm or steal your happiness. Develop empathy for yourself and for others. Doing so will change who you are. In turn, it will have profound and positive impacts on those around you.

True empathy is allowing yourself and others the right to their pain, sorrow, hopes, and dreams. Pain and sorrow allow us to grow and see where some kind of change is needed. The search for change will lead to hopes, dreams, and the possibility that those hopes and dreams can come true. That is a **true** attitude of gratitude. That, my friend, is where your Happily Ever After dwells.

Bad days don't magically disappear. They will always exist, but when you make the **choice** to become grateful, hopeful, and happy, you can choose to focus on the good rather than wallowing in the negative. Put yourself in a position of gratitude. Then, when those minor problems appear, you're set! When major life-changing events happen, you will be ready to handle those unimaginably gut-wrenching moments that appear when you are most vulnerable and when you least expect them.

You will be in a position to allow your mind to open to possibilities and solutions. Your mind will, out of sheer habit, kick in – pushing aside any imaginary disbelief and doom – while helping you find a way to pass through those bad times.

BLOOMING INTO YOUR PURPOSE: BREAKING THROUGH

It all starts with the attitude of gratitude. Give yourself permission to experience gratitude and happiness as part of a practiced daily routine.

I wish I could say I did some right things that day on purpose. I'd like to say that I knew what I was doing was beneficial or that I followed the script to perfection. I cannot.

What I can say is this: It was fortunate that I was already practiced.

While I did let a bad day grow out-of-hand, I am very lucky to have *already* been practicing the attitude of gratitude and empathy. When the chips were down, that practiced way of life took over and put me where I needed to be.

I am much more cautious with my bad days now. I practice feeling them and giving myself permission to have empathy for myself and for others. Then, I practice letting go of the self-pity.

I sincerely hope you will never have an experience similar to the one I just shared. Nevertheless, the truth is that we will all have painful experiences in life – in one form or another. When those experiences come, we always have the **choice** to choose to have empathy for ourselves and others…or hold on to pity and anger.

Your life will be happier and more fulfilling should you **choose** gratitude.

FIND YOUR HAPPILY EVER AFTER NOW...

Harnessing the emotional power during severely traumatic experiences is tough. Harnessing your emotional power will transform your life in a way that nothing else can.

Practice an attitude of gratitude and empathy so that with each opportunity, you will be able to change to a positive and grateful state of mind. Then, you will be able to provide yourself the love that is deserved and the courage to do what you must. You will be able to share hope and love with those around you, too.

That which we focus on expands
and creates
Your *Happily Ever After.*

BLOOMING INTO YOUR PURPOSE: BREAKING THROUGH

Write YOUR own BLOOMING story!

BLOOMING INTO YOUR PURPOSE: BREAKING THROUGH

BLOOMING INTO YOUR PURPOSE: BREAKING THROUGH

BLOOMING INTO YOUR PURPOSE: BREAKING THROUGH

BLOOMING INTO YOUR PURPOSE: BREAKING THROUGH

BLOOMING INTO YOUR PURPOSE: BREAKING THROUGH

BLOOMING INTO YOUR PURPOSE: BREAKING THROUGH

BLOOMING INTO YOUR PURPOSE: BREAKING THROUGH

BLOOMING INTO YOUR PURPOSE: BREAKING THROUGH

BLOOMING INTO YOUR PURPOSE: BREAKING THROUGH

BLOOMING INTO YOUR PURPOSE: BREAKING THROUGH

BLOOMING INTO YOUR PURPOSE: BREAKING THROUGH

Blooming Into Your Purpose: Breaking Through

Authors' Biographies

Darlene Bond is a God-fearing woman who wears many hats: Wife. Mother of three. Daughter. Godmother. Friend. Sister. She was a high-school dropout – the result of giving birth to her first child at the age of 18. She didn't let the circumstance derail her, though; she returned to school and obtained her High School Diploma, Medical Assistant Degree, and Certified Nurse Aide Certification. Presently, she is attending nursing school to become a Licensed Vocational Nurse. A lady of many talents, Darlene is the Owner of several businesses – one of them being a nonprofit organization. She encourages herself and others daily by actively pushing through past pains, hurts, betrayals, and neglect. Darlene states, *"God has a plan for my life. I have been through and seen a lot. I never regret the storms God brought me through. I survived all of them!"*

BLOOMING INTO YOUR PURPOSE: BREAKING THROUGH

La Deema Burns: Wife, Mother, Author, Speaker, Spiritual Life Coach, Visionary, and CEO/Founder of iBloom Movement and Radio. Her passion is to reach out to encourage and empower others with the message that there is healing and hope, in spite of one's brokenness or any of life's other unfortunate circumstances.

Through both the iBloom Movement and iBloom Radio platforms, La Deema sets out to reach churches and ministries to help them impact communities worldwide. She knows it is her divine purpose to share the love of God and see others BLOOM into who God has called them to be while sharing their ministerial messages with the world.

La Deema is a self-published author of *Beauty for Ashes* – an autobiography about molestation, rape, broken family ties, drug addiction, and a failed marriage. She states, "Through all of the brokenness, God was with me – giving me beauty for the ashes of my past life." Today, as a wife and mother of two, La Deema believes family and spiritual strength within the home are paramount.

BLOOMING INTO YOUR PURPOSE: BREAKING THROUGH

Dr. Kim Erwin enjoys her life on North Padre Island where she gets her inspiration for writing. She lives on the water and close to the beach enjoying God's gifts in sunrises, sunsets, and long walks. Her mantra is "God, family, and business". She is mother to Apryl and Nonz and grandmother to Trey. Dr. Erwin is a Eucharistic Minister at The Open Air Church, St. Andrew by the Sea. Her purpose in life is adding value to others.

BLOOMING INTO YOUR PURPOSE: BREAKING THROUGH

"Happily Ever After" Transforming Organizations and the lives of the people within them.

Dr. Karen R. Perkins is an internationally recognized Key Note Speaker, Certified Internal Reset Therapist & Hypnotherapist, Organizational Change & Business Readiness Manager, Trainer, Coach, Consultant, and Author. She's been a C-level Executive and works closely with many other C-level Executives, Entrepreneurs, Millionaires, and Multi-Millionaires and their teams to reach even higher success levels. She's an expert with over 25 years of diversified experience in assisting men and women to better understand themselves, each other, and to surpass their own previous highest expectations. In May 2016, Dr. Perkins' book, *Emotional Power: How to Understand and Use Your Emotions to Propel Yourself to a Better Life*, hit the coveted #1 spot on Amazon's Best Sellers listing as well as the #1 New Release in the Inner-Child Self Help category.

CONNECT WITH LA DEEMA BURNS
CEO / Founder of the iBloom Movement and Radio!

IBloom Movement and Radio Store

(A portion of proceeds from sales goes to help feed the less fortunate and build the iBloom Scholarships for young girls.)

www.customizedgirl.com/s/iBloomMovement

and

shop.spreadshirt.com/iBloomMovementRadio

Email: beautyforashesisa61@gmail.com

Web: **www.ladeemaburns.net**

Facebook: **www.facebook.com/la.deema.burns**

Ministry Facebook Page:

God's Word Speaking Love Into Lives

Twitter: @ladeemaburns

BLOOMING INTO YOUR PURPOSE: BREAKING THROUGH

Available for Kindle and in paperback:

Kindle: www.amazon.com/Beauty-Ashes-Deema-Burns-ebook/dp/B01BYT5UZ0

Paperback: http://www.amazon.com/Beauty-Ashes-Deema-Burns/dp/1514824671

www.ingramcontent.com/pod-product-compliance
Lightning Source LLC
Chambersburg PA
CBHW071530080526
44588CB00011B/1626